Original title: Artus und Excalibur
Text: Angelika Lukesch
Illustrations: Iassen Ghiuselev
English translation: Adapted from a version by Pauline Hejl

First published Great Britain in 1995 by
Macdonald Young Books Ltd
Campus 400
Maylands Avenue
Hemel Hempstead
Herts HP2 7EZ

British Library Cataloguing in Publication Data available.

ISBN: 0 7500 2086 5

Photoset in North Wales by Derek Doyle & Associates, Mold, Clwyd.
Printed in Belgium.

Arthur
and Excalibur

The legend of King Arthur
and the great magic sword

Retold by Angelika Lukesch
Illustrated by Iassen Ghiuselev

MACDONALD YOUNG BOOKS

This is the ancient and mysterious story of King Arthur and the magic sword Excalibur.

Many centuries ago Uther, an ancient King of Britain, died. Uther had no children and nobody knew who would become king. Britain was surrounded by enemies who were waiting for their chance to attack. Without a king, Britain was doomed!

In those days people held a strong belief in the magic power of the 'Lady of the Lake'. This wise woman lived in a temple at the bottom of the Holy Lake. She, too, was worried about the fate of Britain and had found no peace since King Uther's death.

'I must find Britain a king,' she thought and decided to consult her magic mirror.

'Show me who is destined to become King of Britain!' cried the Lady of the Lake, laying her hands on her mirror.

Slowly a picture began to form in the magic mirror and the wise woman saw the face of a young man. She saw that it was Arthur, the foster-child of a nobleman. She nodded thoughtfully. 'So, with my help, the noble Arthur shall become King of England,' she mused, starting to devise a cunning plan.

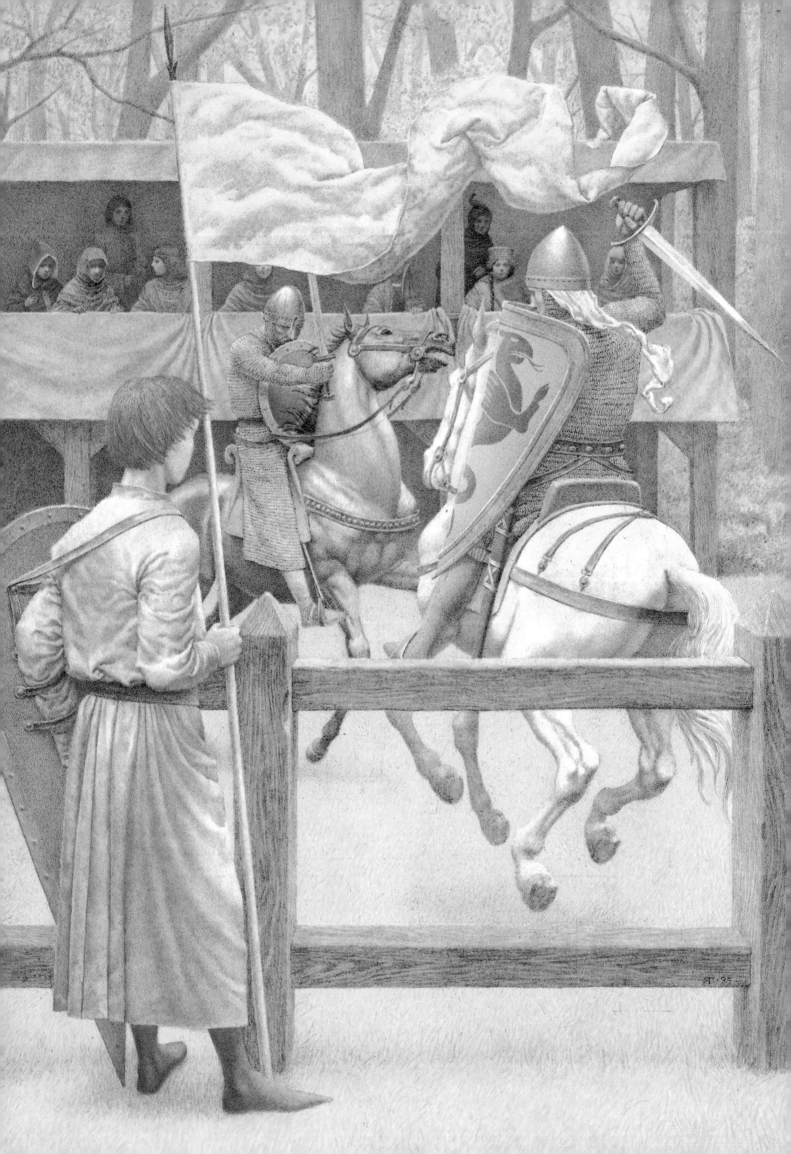

Calling up her magic powers, she forced a magnificent sword into a large forging stone and wrote beneath it the words: 'Whoever pulls this sword from the stone is the rightful King of Britain.'

As soon as the news of the sword in the stone spread around the country, the greatest knights in the land started preparing themselves for this trial of strength. Secretly, each one hoped to become king. The first to step up to the stone was the powerful knight Sir Gawain.

'I'll pull this sword out at a single attempt!' he boasted. He took hold of the sword, sure of victory. But no matter how hard he pulled and tore at the sword, it was to no avail. The sword in the stone did not budge a single jot. Then Sir Gaheris tried his luck. His muscles bulged with the effort and sweat poured from him.

'You damned sword, I'll get you out yet!' he shouted angrily. But all his attempts were in vain. Finally, Sir Gaheris had to give up.

Many other knights tried their strength on the wise woman's sword, but none was able to pull it from the stone.

'We must find a king who will go to war against our enemies,' the noblemen of the land declared. Finally, they decided to arrange a tournament for all the knights. Whoever won would become king.

As the day of the tournament dawned, the most powerful knights in the land came to enter the fray.

The boy Arthur was also there, as a squire. He would have liked to fight too, but he didn't even have a sword! Feeling sad, he walked over to the stone where the Lady of the Lake had planted Excalibur. 'Oh, if only I could pull out this magnificent sword,' thought Arthur, longingly. Then suddenly he noticed the shining figure of a woman standing beside him.

'I am the Lady of the Lake,' she said. 'Pull the sword out, Arthur, I will give you strength. This is a magic sword and its name is Excalibur. As long as it is in your possession, no one will be able to get the better of you. But you must never forget that *I* gave you Excalibur. You can only become king with *my* help.'

Arthur did not know what was happening to him. His hands took hold of the hilt of the sword and, with a single jerk, he pulled it out of the stone! At that very moment, the figure of the Lady of the Lake vanished.

All the knights were astonished when Arthur returned to the tournament with the great sword in his hand. 'Arthur is carrying Excalibur!' the noblemen whispered reverently. They all knelt and shouted joyously: 'Long live King Arthur!'

With much ceremony, Arthur was crowned King of Britain. On the following day, the new king gathered all the knights in the land around him.

'We shall strike fear into the heart of our enemies,' he shouted as his subjects gazed up at him, full of hope.

So King Arthur went to war and soon his army met the foe. The enemy warriors were armed to the teeth, but they hadn't reckoned with the courage of the young king. And they did not know that Arthur had the Lady of the Lake's sword. When his enemies saw how King Arthur swung Excalibur high above his head, they shivered with fear. Deep in their hearts they knew that noone could win against *this* sword.

'Something strange is going on' their leader said to himself when he saw his warriors running away. He flung himself angrily at Arthur, but as soon as Arthur pointed Excalibur at him, he was filled with utter dread. He spurred his horse and fled as quickly as he could. King Arthur was delighted with the easy victory he had had. 'Thanks to Excalibur and the Lady of the Lake, Britain is free!' he shouted.

One day, Arthur met Guinevere, the daughter of
Prince Leodegrans. She was clever and beautiful and
people said she was able to see the Lady of the Lake.

Arthur fell in love with Guinevere and she also took
a great liking to the young king. Soon they were
married and, on their wedding day, Prince Leodegrans
surprised Arthur with a valuable gift. It was a huge
round table with room enough for more than a
hundred knights to sit. Arthur was delighted and
called the brave knights Sir Gawain, Sir Gaheris and
Sir Kay to his side. 'The noblest knights shall sit at my
table,' said Arthur enthusiastically. 'You three shall be
the first Knights of the Round Table!'

King Arthur was not left in peace for long. He soon had to leave Guinevere and his castle, Camelot. His enemies had banded together against him and his kingdom was in danger.

Arthur gathered the Knights of the Round Table and together they set off to war once again. And again it happened that Arthur and his knights came to no harm. With his magic sword in his hand, he and his companions won every battle and frightened off their enemies.

All his success in battle went to King Arthur's head. 'We are the conquerors,' he shouted to his cheering knights after the battle. 'I cannot be beaten!' he said quietly to himself.

He hardly gave the Lady of the Lake a thought.

One day, Queen Guinevere was sitting in the window of her room at Camelot. She was working on some fine embroidery for Excalibur's velvet cover. Guinevere had almost finished her work and was carefully sewing the last threads. She stitched her embroidery onto the velvet cover and was just about to put the sword inside it. But as she touched the sword, she caught sight of the Lady of the Lake!

'Guinevere,' cried the wise woman, 'you are the king's faithful wife, so I give you a warning! If Arthur ever forgets that it is only the magic sword which gives him his powers, it will be taken from him again. He will be killed by his own nephew Mordred.' Guinevere let out a cry of horror as the Lady of the Lake vanished.

From then on Guinevere anxiously watched her beloved husband's every move. She stayed close to him when he came back to Camelot after his battles. Soon she noticed a dangerous change happening to Arthur. He had got used to winning and had become proud and vain. Even his subjects started saying: 'Nobody can do any harm to Arthur. He is almost like a god.'

Arthur had forgotten Excalibur and the Lady of the Lake.

Guinevere was terribly upset. She kept thinking of the wise woman's warning.

'I am his wife, after all,' she said, full of determination, 'I should be able to make him see reason.'

Guinevere found Arthur in the Knights' Hall, sitting on his throne. She spoke to him anxiously. 'My dear husband, we ought to give a token of thanks to the Lady of the Lake. Remember, *she* gave you the magic sword.' Arthur's face became angry. 'Hold your tongue, Guinevere!' he shouted and his eyes became dark with rage. 'Let me tell you once and for all. I am the greatest king of Britain and that has nothing to do with Excalibur or the Lady of the Lake!'

And so disaster took its course . . .

One day King Arthur was out hunting alone. After a while he felt tired and stopped to rest at the edge of the Holy Lake.

When the King had fallen asleep, his nephew Mordred quietly crept up to him and grasped the magic sword. At that moment Arthur awoke.

'Give me my sword,' the King demanded. But Mordred planned to defeat Arthur and become King of Britain himself. Excalibur in hand, he hurled himself at Arthur and tried to kill him. The two of them fought desperately.

Arthur had no way of winning against the great sword. After Mordred had struck him with Excalibur, he fell to his knees, mortally wounded. Just then Arthur saw the of the Lady of the Lake.

'Help me punish Mordred, wise woman!' he called.

Gathering all his strength, he picked up a heavy wooden club and struck Mordred to the ground. Then he collapsed.

In the meantime, Guinevere had run to the Holy Lake, fearing the worst. She found her husband mortally wounded, lying on the bank of the lake next to the dead body of Mordred.

In a weak voice, Arthur said 'I was too proud and ignored the Lady of the Lake. Now Excalibur has been taken from me and rightly so.'

Then the wise woman's voice could be heard once more. She hovered over the lake and stretched out her arms. The magic sword rose up and slid into her hand.

In a serious voice she said 'Excalibur will now return to the bottom of my Holy Lake.' She opened her hand and the sword sank slowly beneath the waves. When her bright form disappeared Arthur could hear her words as he lay dying.

'We will meet again, Arthur! For there is something you must know. In my magic realm you will once more be united with all the Knights of the Round Table and Camelot will live forever!'